Astronomy Now!™

A Look at

SATURN

Suzanne Slade

PowerKiDS
press™

New York

For Don, Odelia, and Donanthony Witt

Published in 2008 by The Rosen Publishing Group, Inc.
29 East 21st Street, New York, NY 10010

First Edition

Editor: Amelie von Zumbusch
Book Design: Greg Tucker
Photo Researcher: Nicole Pristash

Photo Credits: Cover, pp. 13, 15 (top left, top right, bottom left) © NASA/JPL/Space Science Institute; p. 5 by PhotoDisc; p. 7 (main) © Shutterstock.com; pp. 7 (inset), 19 © NASA/JPL; pp. 9; 17, 21 (main) © Getty Images; p. 11 © AFP/Getty Images; p. 13 (top) © Bruce Weaver/AFP/Getty Images; pp. 13 (bottom), 21 (inset) © NASA Kennedy Space Center; p. 15 (bottom right) © HO/AFP/Getty Images.

Library of Congress Cataloging-in-Publication Data

Slade, Suzanne.
  A look at Saturn / Suzanne Slade. — 1st ed.
      p. cm. — (Astronomy now!)
  Includes bibliographical references and index.
  ISBN-13: 978-1-4042-3830-5 (library binding)
  ISBN-10: 1-4042-3830-1 (library binding)
  1. Saturn (Planet)—Juvenile literature. 2. Saturn (Planet)—Satellites—Juvenile literature. 3. Saturn (Planet)—Ring system—Juvenile literature. I. Title.
  QB671.S57 2008
  523.46—dc22
                                              2007008662

Manufactured in the United States of America

3 1967 01039 3240

Contents

Discovering Saturn

Saturn is the second-largest planet in our **solar system**. You can see Saturn at night using only your eyes. It looks like a bright, slow-moving star. Saturn is mostly made of two gases, called **hydrogen** and **helium**. Saturn also has a small amount of **sulfur**, which makes it appear yellow.

Around 700 B.C., the Assyrians were the first people to record seeing Saturn. They called it the Star of Ninib, after one of their gods. They did not know this tiny light was a huge gas planet. The Romans later named the planet Saturn, for one of their gods.

Today, Saturn is best known for the big rings that circle it. However, Saturn's rings were not discovered until the 1600s.

Saturn's Year

Saturn is about 888 million miles (1.4 **billion** km) from the Sun. Saturn is one of the four planets farthest from the Sun. These planets are called the outer planets. The outer planets are made mostly of gas, though **scientists** think they have hard centers.

Saturn is always circling the Sun. The path Saturn travels as it circles the Sun is called its orbit. The length of time it takes a planet to orbit the Sun is that planet's year. Saturn orbits the Sun in about 30 Earth years, so a year on Saturn is about 30 Earth years long.

Saturn's orbit lies between the orbits of the planets Jupiter and Uranus. *Inset:* Saturn, seen here, is the sixth planet from the Sun.

A Day on Saturn

As Saturn orbits the Sun, it also spins. Saturn spins around its axis, a pretend line through the planet's center. Saturn turns so fast that the ends of the planet become flat, making it look like a ball that has lost air.

The time it takes a planet to spin once is its day. Earth's day lasts 24 hours. Scientists had trouble figuring out exactly how long Saturn's day is. This is because Saturn is made of gas, which does not spin evenly. However, scientists used special tools to discover that Saturn's hard center spins around about once every 10 hours and 47 minutes.

Saturn's spinning causes day and night on the planet. It is day on the part of Saturn that faces the Sun. It is night on the part of Saturn that is turned away from the Sun.

Cold and Stormy

You would need lots of warm clothing if you traveled to Saturn. Scientists believe it is about -350° F (-212° C) on Saturn. This is much, much colder than -129° F (-89° C), the coldest **temperature** ever reached on Earth.

Saturn is covered by a thick blanket of gases, called an **atmosphere**. Winds in Saturn's atmosphere travel up to 1,100 miles per hour (1,800 km/h). That is 10 times faster than the wind in Earth's strongest storms. One part of the southern half of Saturn has so many storms that scientists have named it Storm **Alley**.

The bright spots on this picture of Saturn are big storms. The bright circle below Saturn is one of the planet's moons.

Cool Facts

Saturn is known as one of the four gas giants. The other three are Jupiter, Uranus, and Neptune.

The planet Saturn is named after Saturn, a Roman god of farming. Saturn was the father of the Roman god Jupiter.

Many of Saturn's moons are named after the Titans, the giant brothers and sisters of the god Saturn. Others are named after Inuit, French, or Northern European giants.

The rings around Saturn do not travel at the same rate. Scientists are trying to discover why some rings move faster than others.

A Saturn Timeline

2004 – *Cassini-Huygens* becomes the first spacecraft to orbit Saturn.

1977 – *Voyager 1* and *Voyager 2* take off to visit Saturn and other outer planets.

1973 – *Pioneer 11* sets off to visit Saturn and Jupiter.

1659 – Christiaan Huygens suggests that the shapes to the sides of Saturn are rings.

1610 – Galileo Galilei sees strange shapes on either side of Saturn. We now know these shapes were rings.

Fun Figures

Saturn is about 800 million miles (1.3 billion km) from Earth.

Saturn spins on its axis at about 6,200 miles per hour (9,978 km/h).

Though Saturn's rings are many miles (km) wide, they are only about 3,200 feet (1 km) thick.

13

Saturn's Moons

At least 56 moons orbit Saturn. Saturn keeps these moons near with a force called gravity. All large objects in space, such as planets and moons, have gravity. The larger an object is, the more gravity it has. Saturn is 74,898 miles (120,537 km) wide. It is almost 10 times wider than Earth. Therefore, Saturn's gravity is strong. This gravity pulls many moons close and holds them in orbit.

Saturn's closest known moon is named Pan. Pan was discovered by Mark Showalter in 1990. Showalter found this 12-mile- (20 km) wide moon by looking at pictures taken by the *Voyager* spacecraft.

In March 2006, the spacecraft *Cassini* took pictures of icy jets of water spraying high above Saturn's moon Enceladus. Scientists wonder if this means there could be some form of life on Enceladus.

Saturn's moon Mimas is icy and very cold. It is generally about -328° F (-200° C) there.

Hyperion, another of Saturn's moons, is strangely shaped and covered with deep bowl-like landforms called craters that make the moon look like a huge sponge.

Scientists think that Saturn's moon Tethys is mostly made of ice. Tethys has a big crater called Odysseus and a deep valley called Ithaca Chasma.

Giant Titan

Titan, Saturn's largest moon, was discovered by Christiaan Huygens in 1655. Titan is made of ice and rock. It is 3,190 miles (5,134 km) wide. This means Titan is bigger than the planet Mercury! Titan is the second-largest moon in the solar system. Titan is so large that its gravity changes the natural orbit of nearby moons.

The atmosphere around Titan is mostly **nitrogen** gas. This atmosphere is a lot like Earth's atmosphere was long ago. However, Titan's atmosphere is 370 miles (600 km) deep. This is 10 times thicker than Earth's atmosphere.

The weather on Titan, seen here, is very cold. It is generally about -289° F (-178° C) there.

Beautiful Rings

Saturn is best known for its many colorful rings. These beautiful rings were first spotted in 1610, by Galileo Galilei, an Italian scientist who discovered many things about our solar system. Today, scientists have found thousands of different rings circling Saturn.

Saturn's rings are made of pieces of rock and ice. Scientists think these pieces were formed when moons and other space objects broke apart. Saturn's rings are made of so many pieces no one could ever count them all. Some of the pieces are as small as a grain of salt. Other chunks are as big as a house.

Scientists used facts from a spacecraft that visited Saturn to make this picture of its rings. The white bands are the thickest rings. The purple rings are made up of fairly large rocks, while the green ones also have dust.

19

Trips to Saturn

People have asked questions about Saturn for hundreds of years. Today, scientists send off spacecraft to visit Saturn and answer these questions. The first spacecraft to **explore** Saturn was *Pioneer 11*. It blasted off in 1973 and reached Saturn in 1979. *Pioneer 11* came within 22,000 miles (35,406 km) of Saturn. It took pictures and found a new ring.

In the 1980s, *Voyager 1* and *Voyager 2* flew past Saturn. *Voyager 1* gave scientists clues about how Saturn's rings were formed. *Voyager 2* gathered facts about Saturn's moons. It explored Enceladus, a bright, smooth moon, and Phoebe, a dark, bumpy moon.

Voyager 2 took this picture of Saturn and its rings. *Inset:* On September 5, 1977, *Voyager 1* took off from Cape Canaveral, Florida. It visited both Jupiter and Saturn.

Exploring Saturn

A spacecraft named *Cassini-Huygens* arrived at Saturn in 2004. Part of this craft, called *Huygens*, left the main ship and landed on Titan. *Huygens* made important discoveries about Titan's soil and atmosphere. The remaining part of the spacecraft, named *Cassini*, took close-up pictures of Saturn's storms. *Cassini* continued to orbit Saturn and send facts and pictures back to Earth.

In coming years, scientists will search for life on Titan. They also want to learn more about Saturn's moon Enceladus because *Cassini* found water there. Scientists have just begun to discover the many interesting secrets Saturn holds.

Glossary

alley (A-lee) A small street.

atmosphere (AT-muh-sfeer) The gases around an object in space.

billion (BIL-yun) A thousand millions.

explore (ek-SPLOR) To travel over a little-known area.

helium (HEE-lee-um) A light, colorless gas.

hydrogen (HY-dreh-jen) A colorless gas that burns easily and weighs less than any other known kind of matter.

nitrogen (NY-truh-jen) A gas without taste or color that can be found in the air.

scientists (SY-un-tists) People who study the world.

solar system (SOH-ler SIS-tem) A group of planets that circles a star.

sulfur (SUL-fur) A kind of yellow matter that can be found in all living things.

temperature (TEM-pur-cher) How hot or cold something is.

Index

Web Sites

Due to the changing nature of Internet links, PowerKids Press has developed an online list of Web sites related to the subject of this book. This site is updated regularly. Please use this link to access the list: www.powerkidslinks.com/astro/saturn/